SHARKS SET II

THRESHER SHARKS

Adam G. Klein
ABDO Publishing Company

visit us at
www.abdopub.com

Published by ABDO Publishing Company, 4940 Viking Drive, Edina, Minnesota 55435.
Copyright © 2006 by Abdo Consulting Group, Inc. International copyrights reserved in all
countries. No part of this book may be reproduced in any form without written permission from
the publisher. The Checkerboard Library™ is a trademark and logo of ABDO Publishing
Company.

Printed in the United States.

Cover Photo: © Doug Perrine / SeaPics.com
Interior Photos: Corbis pp. 13, 19; © Doug Perrine / SeaPics.com pp. 11, 21; © Jason Isley /
    SeaPics.com p. 5; © Marilyn & Maris Kazmers / SeaPics.com p. 17; © Marty Snyderman /
    SeaPics.com p. 16; © Michael Leonard / SeaPics.com p. 9; © Stephen Kajiura / SeaPics.com
    p. 15; Uko Gorter pp. 6-7

Series Coordinator: Heidi M. Dahmes
Editors: Heidi M. Dahmes, Megan M. Gunderson
Art Direction: Neil Klinepier

Library of Congress Cataloging-in-Publication Data

Klein, Adam G., 1976-
    Thresher sharks / Adam G. Klein.
        p. cm. -- (Sharks. Set II)
    Includes bibliographical references.
    ISBN 1-59679-290-6
    1. Alopiidae--Juvenile literature. 2. Sharks--Juvenile literature. I. Title.

QL638.95.A4K54 2006
597.3--dc22
                                                        2005045291

CONTENTS

THRESHER SHARKS AND FAMILY

Sharks are some of the most feared sea creatures. But, they are fascinating to learn about. There are more than 200 species of sharks. They swim through every ocean in the world.

Several features help sharks swim with more ease. Sharks are made of **cartilage**, which is lighter than bone. They also have oily **livers**. This oil is lighter than water. And, a shark's fins and tail are designed to propel it through the water.

Sharks share many other common features. They have toothlike scales called **dermal denticles** covering their skin. These denticles are a protective covering for the shark.

Sharks are carnivores.
So, they eat meat. Most
sharks eat live fish.

There are three species of thresher sharks. These
are the thresher, the bigeye thresher, and the pelagic
thresher. Each species has the large tail typical of a
thresher shark. They are strong, active swimmers. They
are most often found near the surface of the water.

What They Look Like

Thresher sharks are stocky fish with large eyes. They have a short, pointed snout and a short head. They have long, narrow **pectoral** fins and a large front **dorsal** fin. And, their teeth are small and bladelike.

CAUDAL (TAIL) FIN

Thresher sharks have a dark back and a light belly. The color on their backs blends into spots on their undersides near the tail. This color pattern helps hide these sharks in the water.

The average thresher shark is 18 to 20 feet (5 to 6 m) long. The bigeye thresher is smaller. Its maximum length is about 15 feet (5 m). And, the pelagic thresher only reaches a maximum size of about 11 feet (3 m).

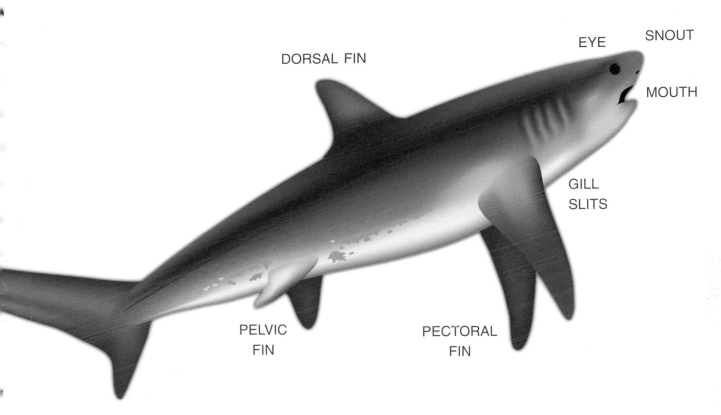

DORSAL FIN

EYE

SNOUT

MOUTH

GILL
SLITS

PELVIC
FIN

PECTORAL
FIN

The most obvious way to identify a thresher shark is by its giant tail. The tail of the thresher makes up about half of its body length. Thresher sharks use their powerful tails in combination with their large front fins for swimming. They also use their tails for hunting.

WHERE THEY LIVE

Thresher sharks live throughout the oceans of the world. They occupy **temperate** to tropical regions of the Atlantic, Pacific, and Indian oceans. They are most often found close to shore. But, they can also be found very far out to sea.

Young thresher sharks often travel into bays. Adult thresher sharks are common over the **continental shelf**. Thresher sharks can be found up to 1,200 feet (370 m) below the surface. And, bigeye threshers have been found as deep as 1,640 feet (500 m).

Throughout the year, thresher sharks **migrate** many miles. During the summer months, thresher sharks can be found far from the equator. Water temperatures are warm enough for them to live as far north as Norway. During the winter, they return to waters near the equator.

Thresher sharks are known to leap out of the water. It takes a very powerful creature to jump completely out of the water. This is even more amazing because of the thresher shark's massive size.

Food

In nature, animals use their natural abilities for survival. A thresher shark's greatest gift for survival is its tail. Thresher sharks hunt schools of fish by swimming in circles around them.

When hunting, the thresher shark uses its tail to herd the fish together. Then, the shark slaps its tail. That slapping action stuns some of the fish in the school. The shark feeds on the stunned fish. It is an effective way for a creature to use its natural abilities to capture a meal.

Sometimes thresher sharks hunt in pairs. Instead of competing, the sharks help each other. Each shark will take turns swiping through the school of fish. The sharks will keep at it until the school is too small to supply any more food.

The main sources of food for thresher sharks are these schools of fish. Other times, a meal has to come from a wider variety of creatures. Thresher sharks also feed on squid and octopuses.

Thresher sharks spend most of their time near the water's surface. That is where their food is.

SENSES

Sharks have some senses similar to humans. Thresher sharks have well-developed eyes. They have a strong sense of smell that works underwater. And, they have a keen sense of hearing that helps them find prey.

Sharks also have unique senses. Thresher sharks can sense vibrations with their lateral line system. They have fluid-filled canals running down each side of their bodies. These canals detect sounds and water movement.

Sharks have special sensory **pores** in their heads called ampullae of Lorenzini. These pores detect electrical charges in the water. Living creatures give off charges, which sharks can use to locate them.

Thresher sharks also have the ability to detect pressure changes in the water. Pressure changes tell them the water depth. By using all of their senses, these sharks can understand their surroundings and find their next meal.

Bigeye threshers are named for their enormous eyes.

BABIES

It takes about 14 years for thresher sharks to become mature enough for mating. This is due to the slow growth rate of many large shark species.

Thresher sharks are **ovoviviparous**. So, the eggs remain inside the mother after they are fertilized. As they develop, each **embryo** lives off the nourishment inside its egg. Eventually the yolk in the egg runs out. Then, the embryos have to find another source for food.

Throughout the **pregnancy**, the mother shark continues to release eggs. The embryos eat these eggs as well as smaller embryos in order to survive.

Mother thresher sharks birth two to four young at a time. Baby sharks are called pups. These pups are well developed and ready for life. Baby sharks do not remain near their mothers. The mother swims away soon after her pups are born.

Bigeye threshers are about 24 to 48 inches (61 to 122 cm) long at birth. The pelagic thresher is about 39 inches (99 cm) long. Thresher shark pups are the largest. They are born between 48 and 60 inches (122 and 152 m) long.

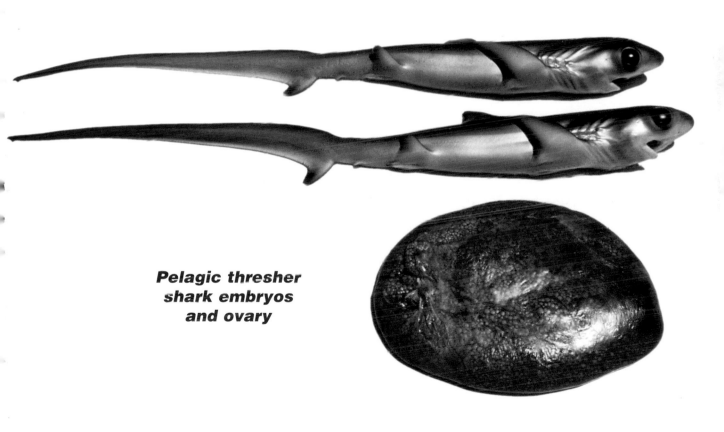

Pelagic thresher shark embryos and ovary

ATTACK AND DEFENSE

Thresher sharks use their body coloring as a form of defense. Their bodies blend into the water whether viewed from above or below. Being hidden helps these sharks sneak up on prey and hide from **predators**.

Larger sharks prey on young thresher sharks. But, adult thresher sharks have no natural predators. Their biggest enemies are humans. The thresher shark's long tail often gets them hooked by fishers.

This thresher shark is caught in a gill net. These nets are invisible to a shark. The shark swims into the net and becomes caught by its head or gills.

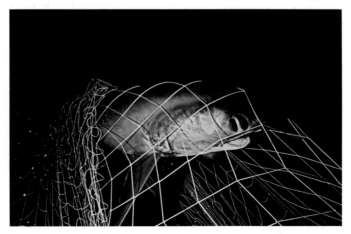

Thresher sharks are hunted commercially and for sport. Their meat is used for food, and their skin is used for leather. A shark's **liver** is a source of vitamins and oil. In some cultures, shark fin soup is a popular meal.

Thresher sharks also battle **parasites**. Parasites attach to the thresher shark's gill filaments and can cause damage. This damage can lead to breathing problems.

Thresher sharks are a favorite of sportfishers because they are strong, active swimmers.

ATTACKS ON HUMANS

Many people fear sharks. But, sharks do not naturally prey on humans. Sharks do attack humans sometimes. But in the United States, the risk of being killed by lightning is 30 times greater than being killed in a shark attack.

Sharks attack humans for different reasons. A shark may feel threatened and try to protect itself. Or, a shark may be looking for its next meal. People are found at the surface where many sharks find their food. And, humans create movements that sharks can detect.

Thresher sharks are not **aggressive** creatures. They prefer to shy away from people. So, they are not considered harmful. But, because of their large size and their strong tail, thresher sharks should be avoided.

When viewed from below, this person floating in a raft looks like a marine animal. A shark could mistake this person for food and attack.

THRESHER SHARK FACTS

Scientific Name:

Thresher shark	*Alopias vulpinus*
Bigeye thresher shark	*A. superciliosus*
Pelagic thresher shark	*A. pelagicus*

Average Size:

The average thresher shark is 18 to 20 feet (5 to 6 m) long. The length of a bigeye thresher is normally between 11 and 13 feet (3 and 4 m). The pelagic thresher is about 8 to 10 feet (2 to 3 m) long.

Where They're Found:

Thresher sharks live in temperate to tropical regions of the Atlantic, Pacific, and Indian oceans.

Thresher sharks are often hooked by their tails. This is probably because they are trying to stun a fisher's bait.

GLOSSARY

aggressive - displaying hostility.

cartilage (KAHR-tuh-lihj) - the soft, elastic connective tissue in the skeleton. A person's nose and ears are made of cartilage.

continental shelf - a shallow, underwater plain that borders a continent and ends with a steep slope to the ocean floor.

dermal denticle - a small toothlike projection on a shark's skin.

dorsal - located near or on the back, especially of an animal.

embryo - an organism in the early stages of development.

liver - a large organ that produces bile, stores carbohydrates, and performs other bodily functions.

migrate - to move from one place to another, often to find food.

ovoviviparous (OH-voh-veye-VIH-puh-ruhs) - a fish or reptile that carries its eggs inside it while they develop.

parasite - an organism that lives off of another organism of a different species.

pectoral - located in or on the chest.

pore - a small opening in an animal or plant through which matter passes.

predator - an animal that kills and eats other animals.

pregnant - having one or more babies growing within the body.

temperate - having neither very hot nor very cold weather.

WEB SITES

To learn more about thresher sharks, visit ABDO Publishing Company on the World Wide Web at **www.abdopub.com**. Web sites about thresher sharks are featured on our Book Links page. These links are routinely monitored and updated to provide the most current information available.

INDEX

A

ampullae of Lorenzini
    12
Atlantic Ocean 8
attacks 18

B

belly 6
body 6, 7, 12, 16

C

cartilage 4
color 6, 16

D

defense 4, 6, 16, 18
dermal denticles 4

E

eggs 14
eyes 6, 12

F

fins 4, 6, 7, 17
food 10, 11, 12, 14,
    16, 18

H

head 6, 12
hunting 7, 10, 12, 16

I

Indian Ocean 8

L

lateral line 12
liver 4, 17

M

mating 14
migration 8

N

Norway 8

O

oil 4, 17

P

Pacific Ocean 8
parasites 17
predators 16, 17
pups 14, 15

S

senses 12, 18
shark species 4, 14
size 6, 7, 15, 18
skin 4, 17
snout 6

T

tail 4, 5, 6, 7, 10, 16,
    18
teeth 6

U

United States 18